Our Good Teachers

What The Real Experts Are Saying About Education

Carolyn Clay Oliver, Ed.D.
and Ellen Reilly McCormick

Illustrated by Students
Cover Illustration: Emma Fuller, 7th Grade

Good Teacher, Inc.
Richmond, VA

Design: Good Teacher, Inc.

Good Teacher, Inc.
P.O. Box 14794
Richmond, VA 23221

Manufactured in the USA
First Printing March 1995

ISBN 0-9629972-5-0

"A good teacher is a good person that teaches someone."

To Susie Hickman, who reawakened my passion for teaching and learning by opening my eyes to the possibilities and power of a good teacher's influence on students and their families.

To Debbie Miller, Clay's world-class third grade teacher, who lives on every page and continues to be my good teacher, editor, advisor and friend.

And to all good teachers everywhere whose commitment to your students' learning and growth is as immeasurable as your impact.

–CCO

In loving memory of my father, Charles A. Reilly, mentor, teacher, and school principal.

–ERM

Dear Children:

This is the first of many pages we have saved for you to write and draw something special for your teacher. Whenever you see apples marching in this book, it is *your* time to be the author and illustrator. Have fun!

Love Oliver

Ellen McCormick

Jan. 1997

For <u>My friend, Dorothy</u>

From <u>Frankie Lynn</u>
With Love!

You are a good teacher because...
you care so very much —
you believe that every
   child can learn —
you give it your all
   every single day —

A good teacher opens my eyes to this whole planet.

A good teacher s t r e t c h e s my mind.

A good teacher remembers I am left-handed.

A good teacher knows what we'll be doing next Thursday.

"She's focused. She knows exactly what she's doing, exactly what she wants to do; yet she's open to all kinds of 'hows.'"

Colleague

A good teacher knows how I learn best.

A good teacher tells us when she's proud of us.

A good teacher helps us understand that everybody's best is not the same.

"She has challenged and yet she has not pushed the children to be more than who they are."
Parent

A good teacher has me find my own mistakes.

Being Nice to Others

Super

Clay 4/2/9[?]

Being nice to others is
not comenting alot it just
is treating them like one of your
best friends even when they
aren't. A best friend is someone you care about alot and
hope the best for them. If
you treat them nice and
they don't the geschin is why do
you give your repect to them.

"Children become good writers by writing. I have my students write all the time because writing ties everything together. Seeing me write with them validates their writing."
A Good Teacher

A good teacher writes with us.

A good teacher gives me an awesome choice of vegetables when I won't be a mushroom in the school play.

"She can always find each child's comfort zone, where he or she can be comfortable without feeling silly or embarrassed."

Parent

Dd Ee Ff Gg Hh Ii Jj
Schedule
Math - 9:00
P.E. - 10:30
Recess - 12:30
Writing 1:00
eading - 2:00
School Play
tomato = Bobby
celery
mushroom
carrot
avocado
egg plant = Charmian
broccoli
Homework
Math - pg 192, 1-15
Writing
Reading -

Good

Super

WOW

A good teacher tells me when I do a good job

and

Wonderful

"The children feel her excitement. She wants everything in that classroom for the good of those children."

Colleague

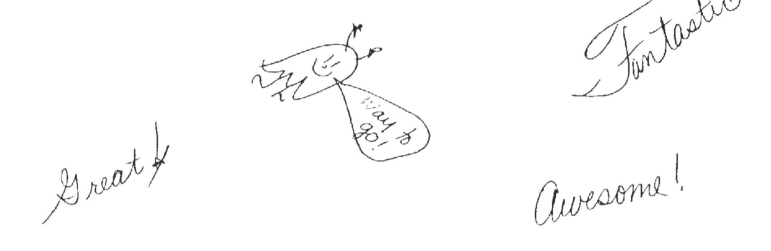

Great!

Fantastic

Awesome!

celebrates with me when I learn something new.

Terrific

Smile

A good teacher makes me glad to be me.

"She makes everybody feel like the best person."
Student

"I hope the confidence is something she's built inside that can't go away."
Parent

A good teacher is glad to see my parents—and they know it.

A good teacher's voice keeps telling me,

> "Do your best.
>
> I know you can.
>
> Do your very best."

"My child has no fear of failure. I think that's the best thing you can give a child. And she always has that little process challenging the kids, saying to them 'can we go one step farther?'"

Parent

Do your best

Do your best

Do your best

Do your best

Bear

"That's what parents and good teachers do, we remember things they say, they help you become stronger the older you get."

Student

Aa Bb Cc Dd Ee Ff G

A good teacher listens to everyone's ideas.

"The most important requirement for a teacher is that he or she listen, really listen to each child, and absorb it, and think about what that child is saying. Sometimes there are a lot of meanings in a question a child will ask."

Parent

A good teacher helps us talk about stuff that worries us.

"...And makes us feel safe. Safe is never scared, you never feel scared inside and you have no doubts."

Student

A good teacher gives me t   i   m   e   to answer her questions.

"It's important to give a child time to think before you move on to another child for an answer. Giving him time says 'I value your trying to figure out an answer.' Speed is not what I'm trying to teach; thinking is."

A Good Teacher

A good teacher pays attention too.

A good teacher helps me discover exciting places.

"You can stand outside the door and listen. They <u>cannot</u> <u>wait</u> to contribute to the discussion and ask questions."

Parent

A good teacher knows everybody has a bad day now and then.

A good teacher knows when *I'm* having a bad day.

A good teacher is happy to see me every morning.

A good teacher lets me play outside
when it's cold.

A good teacher wants us all to have fun in gym class.

A good teacher looks into my eyes when we're talking.

Aa Bb Cc Dd
Happy Birthday Billy
NOW DOES EVERYONE UNDERSTAND GRAVITY?
Gravity

A good teacher SHOWS us.

A good teacher knows when I'm embarrassed.

*"I like the way you understand
when somebody hurts my feelings."*
Student

A good teacher helps me hunt for my retainer.

A good teacher gets me thinking in other directions.

A good teacher makes every day important.

A good teacher knows all families are real families.

A good teacher is patient when I can't remember

"I like the way you're patient and have so much confidence in us. You expect us to do well so we expect us to do well."

Student

which way the "b" goes.

A good teacher teaches us to teach each other.

A good teacher learns from US.

A good teacher reminds me to water my science project before it's too late.

A good teacher loves my presents.

A good teacher acts the same around the principal,

the custodian,

the school nurse,

and other teachers.

A good teacher is nice to all the kids in school.

A good teacher smiles and winks when I'm on stage and feeling
very nervous.

*"She invests extreme confidence
and love in these children and she
makes them shine!"*
                    Parent

A good teacher likes ALL our pets.

A good teacher celebrates all our holidays.

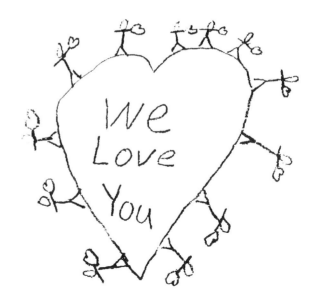

A good teacher laughs at my knock-knock jokes.

A good teacher gets dirty on field trips.

A good teacher respects
my projects.

A good teacher asks me

HOW

so I can figure out WHY.

A good teacher makes sure I know what's going on.

"I always have in the back of my mind (or the front of my mind) my goals for each individual and for the total class."

A Good Teacher

A good teacher wants us all to have our dreams.

"You've got to make children believe they can do anything – while recognizing that they can't do everything. If they do believe in themselves they'll take the risks."

A Good Teacher

A good teacher mixes math and reading
and spelling
and music
and science
together.

A good teacher makes Mozart come alive.

A good teacher makes me WANT to read.

A good teacher laughs when things are funny and doesn't laugh when things aren't funny.

A good teacher lets me go to the nurse
when I'm sick.

A good teacher makes me forget I am learning.

A good teacher makes things that happened a long time ago interesting and not boring.

A good teacher helps me explore.

A good teacher wants to know what I think.

"I have a responsibility to help my kids grow in all dimensions, teaching them to be independent, and encouraging them to care about others, be honest, the whole plane. It's all really, really important – just as important as the academic skills."
A Good Teacher

A good teacher listens to all sides. A good teacher listens to all sides.

A good teacher listens to all sides. A good

A good teacher listens to all sides. A good

teacher listens to all sides. A good teacher listens to all sides.

A good teacher helps us learn to treat each other with respect.

"When I'm on playground duty I can see a difference with her class; they're out there sticking up for each other and having fun and not arguing."
                Colleague

"Other classes don't care about each other like we do, unless they have a best friend in there."
Students

It's good to have a good teacher.

Dear _____

You're my good teacher because . . .

_____

_____

_____

_____

Sincerely,

_____

AUTHOR'S NOTE

"A good teacher is a good person who teaches somebody," said one of our young contributors to this book. And thusly I thank all of my good teachers who happen to be children. You have touched my life in profound measure since my career as a professional educator began more than 20 years ago.

I will always be indebted to the second graders from Susie Hickman's class during the 1989-90 school year. Now seventh graders, these children offered me their disarming wisdom about teachers and learning. All I had to do was ask—and listen. It is their voices who spoke to you in *A Good Teacher*, my first book published in 1991, and whose words continue to ring with clarity and truth throughout these pages.

When I decided to revise *A Good Teacher*, I did so believing that the powerful observations of children required equally powerful illustrations. I went back to the experts—students—and asked for their help.

All of the student-illustrators, ages 6 to 14, who offered their art and ideas for *Our Good Teachers* have my deepest gratitude. Your drawings and personal observations of your own good teachers have added texture and feeling to the entire work.

-*CCO*, February, 1995